HAL•LEONARD®
VIOLIN
PLAY-ALONG

AUDIO
ACCESS
INCLUDED

Lindsey Stirling
FAVORITES

PLAYBACK+
Speed • Pitch • Balance • Loop

To access audio visit:
www.halleonard.com/mylibrary

Enter Code
6402-9744-9320-7466

Photo by Noam Galai/Getty Images

ISBN 978-1-4950-6287-2

Jon Vriesacker, violin
Audio arrangements by Andrew Horowitz
Audio arrangements for "Mission: Impossible Theme"
and "Who Wants to Live Forever" by Peter Deneff
Recorded and Produced by Jake Johnson at Paradyme Productions

7777 W. BLUEMOUND RD. P.O. BOX 13819 MILWAUKEE, WI 53213

Visit Hal Leonard Online at
www.halleonard.com

HAL•LEONARD®
VIOLIN
PLAY-ALONG

AUDIO
ACCESS
INCLUDED

Lindsey Stirling
FAVORITES

CONTENTS

Assassin's Creed III Main Title

By Lorne Blafe
Arranged by Lindsey Stirling

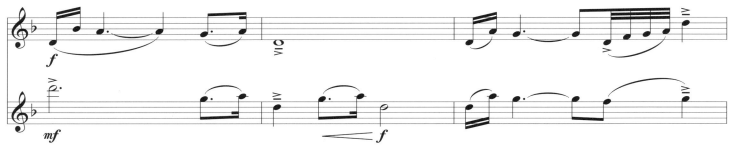

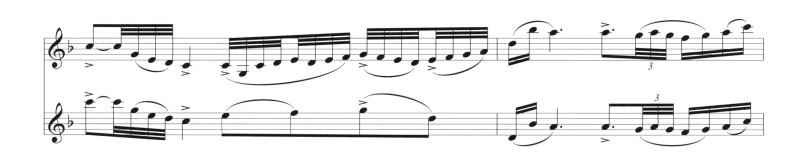

Game of Thrones

Theme from the HBO Series GAME OF THRONES
Music by Ramin Djawadi
Arranged by Lindsey Stirling and Peter Hollens

Grenade

Words and Music by Bruno Mars, Ari Levine, Philip Lawrence, Brody Brown, Claude Kelly and Andrew Wyatt
Arranged by Lindsey Stirling, Alex Boye and Nathaniel Drew

Hallelujah

Words and Music by Leonard Cohen
Arranged by Lindsey Stirling

daintily, with anticipation and excitement

with resolve

solo, reverently

rall.

Mission: Impossible Theme

from the Paramount Television Series MISSION: IMPOSSIBLE
By Lalo Schifrin
Arranged by Lindsey Stirling and The Piano Guys

Pure Imagination

from WILLY WONKA AND THE CHOCOLATE FACTORY

Words and Music by Leslie Bricusse and Anthony Newley
Arranged by Lindsey Stirling and Josh Groban

Who Wants to Live Forever

Words and Music by Brian May
Arranged by The Tenors and Lindsey Stirling

Take Me Home

Words and Music by Samuel Frisch, Brandon Lowry, Alex Makhlouf, Jean Paul Makhlouf and Bleta Rexha
Arranged by Lindsey Stirling